I0161138

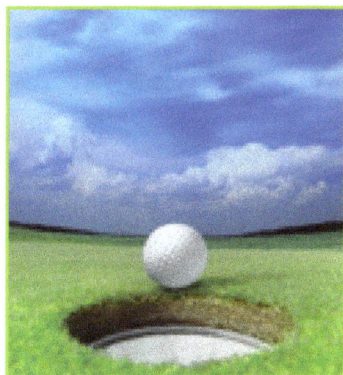

Join Clickit Golf and Receive a Free Mobile App!

Send an email to support@clickitgolf.com and write in the subject line, "Book Promo." Clickit Golf will then create a golf mobile app for your course (valued at $199).

Register your course for free to join Clickit Golf and over one million golfers who annually visit Clickit Golf to book their discounted tee times.

Driving Incremental Golf Course Revenue

Tee up your winning business strategy for generating incremental revenue for your golf course

Jeff Shavitz

THiNKaha®
An Actionable Business Journal

E-mail: info@thinkaha.com
20660 Stevens Creek Blvd., Suite 210
Cupertino, CA 95014

Published by THiNKaha®
20660 Stevens Creek Blvd., Suite 210, Cupertino, CA 95014
http://thinkaha.com
E-mail: info@thinkaha.com

First Printing: June 2017
Hardcover ISBN: 978-1-61699-203-3 1-61699-203-4
Paperback ISBN: 978-1-61699-204-0 1-61699-204-2
eBook ISBN: 978-1-61699-205-7 1-61699-205-0
Place of Publication: Silicon Valley, California, USA
Paperback Library of Congress Number: 2016961251

Trademarks

All terms mentioned in this book that are known to be trademarks or service marks have been appropriately capitalized. Neither THiNKaha, nor any of its imprints, can attest to the accuracy of this information. Use of a term in this book should not be regarded as affecting the validity of any trademark or service mark.

Warning and Disclaimer

Every effort has been made to make this book as complete and as accurate as possible. The information provided is on an "as is" basis. The author(s), publisher, and their agents assume no responsibility for errors or omissions. Nor do they assume liability or responsibility to any person or entity with respect to any loss or damages arising from the use of information contained herein.

Dedication

Dedicated to my partner, David Moore, for introducing me to Clickit Golf, Inc. and the business of golf. I never thought I would be so fortunate to work in the industry of a sport I love so much.

I also want to dedicate this book to my parents, wife, and three children, as we have shared special moments together on the golf course. What other sport enables three generations of a family to spend four hours of quality time together?

Acknowledgement

All of us who love the game of golf are nuts about our sport. Aren't you? Whether it's the golf executive, the head pro, groundskeepers, caddies, and of course, the golfers, I want to acknowledge all of us for finding a passion we love that we also want to share with our friends and family!

How to Read a THiNKaha® Book
A Note from the Publisher

The THiNKaha series is the CliffsNotes of the 21st century. The value of these books is that they are contextual in nature. Although the actual words won't change, their meaning will change every time you read one as your context will change. Experience your own "AHA!" moments ("AHAmessages™") with a THiNKaha book; AHAmessages are looked at as "actionable" moments—think of a specific project you're working on, an event, a sales deal, a personal issue, etc. and see how the AHAmessages in this book can inspire your own AHAmessages, something that you can specifically act on. Here's how to read one of these books and have it work for you:

1. Read a THiNKaha book (these slim and handy books should only take about 15–20 minutes of your time!) and write down one to three actionable items you thought of while reading it. Each journal-style THiNKaha book is equipped with space for you to write down your notes and thoughts underneath each AHAmessage.

2. Mark your calendar to re-read this book again in 30 days.

3. Repeat step #1 and write down one to three more AHAmessages that grab you this time. I guarantee that they will be different than the first time. BTW: this is also a great time to reflect on the actions taken from the last set of AHAmessages you wrote down.

After reading a THiNKaha book, writing down your AHAmessages, re-reading it, and writing down more AHAmessages, you'll begin to see how these books contextually apply to you. THiNKaha books advocate for continuous, lifelong learning. They will help you transform your AHAs into actionable items with tangible results until you no longer have to say "AHA!" to these moments—they'll become part of your daily practice as you continue to grow and learn.

As The AHA Guy at THiNKaha, I definitely practice what I preach. I read 2-3 AHAbooks a month in addition to those that we publish and take away two to three different action items from each of them every time. Please e-mail me your AHAs today!

Mitchell Levy
publisher@thinkaha.com

THiNKaha®

Contents

Section I
Running a Golf Course   11

Section II
Selling to the Golf Consumer   25

Section III
Non-traditional Golf Course Revenue   43

Section IV
Your Employees Matter   57

Section V
Don't Be Afraid of Technology   71

Section VI
Know Your Numbers   83

Section VII
AHAs to Think About   95

About the Author   117

SECTION

I

Running a Golf Course

Business is business whether you're running a golf course or any other type of company. In this section, we will outline standard business principles that are relevant for all business owners, regardless of industry.

1

Ideas are relatively easy to think of –
it's the execution that's hard. @JeffShavitz

_____

_____

_____

2

Do you love or like what you do?
Most people don't love it, but you can
be one of the few who do if you plan
accordingly. @JeffShavitz

_____

_____

_____

3

You're simply not the master of your life when working for corporate America, and the ultimate payoff is out of your control. @JeffShavitz

_____

_____

_____

4

Running a golf course is very similar to running any business – your office just has a much prettier backyard. @JeffShavitz

_____

_____

_____

5

When you own a golf course, when it's good, it's great, and when it's bad, it really sucks! @JeffShavitz

_____

_____

_____

6

GADD: Golf Attention Deficit Disorder – I have it, do you? Focus each day on your priorities. @JeffShavitz

_____

_____

_____

7

Be patient: creating a successful golf course rarely happens overnight. Same as learning golf takes years to master. @JeffShavitz

_____

_____

_____

8

Have you already thought of your "exit strategy" before buying your golf course? Enjoy the journey, the exit will come. @JeffShavitz

_____

_____

_____

9

Do the business tasks that you hate doing first thing in the morning. By 10:30AM, you should be done with this work. @JeffShavitz

_____

_____

_____

10

Decisions, decisions, and more decisions – as a business owner, you better be prepared to make them and make them quickly. @JeffShavitz

_____

_____

_____

11

Have you completed your business and vision statement? Is it all fluff? Or does it mean something special for your course? @JeffShavitz

_____

_____

_____

12

If you are doing administrative tasks not par with "your greatest value," hire an assistant to do it for you. Time is money. @JeffShavitz

_____

_____

_____

13

Networking & Networking: Most people do it all wrong. Study your "ROT" (Return on Time) vs. your ROI (Return on Investment). @JeffShavitz

_____

_____

_____

14

Branding is very different than marketing for your golf course; make sure you understand the difference. @JeffShavitz

_____

_____

_____

15

Death by over-planning – at some point, just get out there and start. @JeffShavitz

_____

_____

_____

16

Golf professionals need to work "on" their golf business plan and not "in" their golf business. @JeffShavitz

_____

_____

_____

17

Don't buy a golf course only because you love golf. With this logic, all your golfing buddies would own a golf course. @JeffShavitz

_____

_____

_____

18

Helping with nonprofits and other philanthropic causes will make you a better human being and your golf course thrive.
@JeffShavitz

_____

_____

_____

19

You must define what success means for your facility –without a clear definition, you will never know if you achieve success.
@JeffShavitz

_____

_____

_____

SECTION

II

Selling to the Golf Consumer

Without customers, you don't have a successful golf course business. Learn different ways to create an authentic and real relationship with your customers and incent them to play many of rounds of golf at your course.

20

We all need customers, we all need traffic. All businesses are the same, whether golf or anything else. @JeffShavitz

_____

_____

_____

21

Nothing happens without sales.
Don't forget those four simple words.
@JeffShavitz

_____

_____

_____

22

Without golfers, you have no golf business. It's a simple fact and don't ever forget that! @JeffShavitz

_____

_____

_____

23

Golf is a lifestyle business. Have fun with your customers and the industry at large. @JeffShavitz

_____

_____

_____

24

Golf is an amazing way to spend the afternoon building relationships with your customers. @JeffShavitz

_____

_____

_____

25

How can you continue to attract
new golfers to your course? @JeffShavitz

_____

_____

_____

26

Attrition is the killer word – you want your
golfers coming back for future rounds!
@JeffShavitz

_____

_____

_____

27

If you want golfers coming back, keep your offers fresh. Think what your golfers want!
@JeffShavitz

_____

_____

_____

28

Diagnose your golfers' needs and present products and services to meet those needs – pretty simple philosophy. @JeffShavitz

_____

_____

_____

29

When was the last time you called your customer to ask how their golfing experience was? Never? Start today! @JeffShavitz

_____

_____

_____

30

When was the last time you truly thanked your golfers for coming to your course. Have you ever? Try a physical thank you note. @JeffShavitz

_____

_____

_____

31

Show your appreciation & write thank you notes. The handwritten note is a lost art: pick up a pen & paper & send it US Mail. @JeffShavitz

_____

_____

_____

32

Pick up the phone, and call a minimum of three existing customers to thank them for their business and check in to say hello. @JeffShavitz

_____

_____

_____

33

Know your customers' birthdays
& give a free beer, range balls &
round of golf on their special day.
It will go a long way! @JeffShavitz

_____

_____

_____

34

Customers would rather buy a good
product from an extraordinary company
than an extraordinary product from a bad
company. @JeffShavitz

_____

_____

_____

35

Play golf with your clients: it creates an immediate connection that will not easily be replicated by the competition. @JeffShavitz

_____

_____

_____

36

Customers have a hard time finding great courses to play. Don't sell yourself short and charge a competitive price. @JeffShavitz

_____

_____

_____

37

How many trade-shows and/or conventions do you attend each year? Make it more than four: get out and meet some new people. @JeffShavitz

_____

_____

_____

38

Golf is not going away – you must be creative in getting the players to your course. @JeffShavitz

_____

_____

_____

39

The Law of Reciprocity works in golf, business & life. If you help someone, it come back in a positive way. It works! @JeffShavitz

_____

_____

_____

40

Targeted emails twice per week to local golfers is an effective way to drive more weekend round sales. @JeffShavitz

_____

_____

_____

41

Emailing your golf database is very powerful. But you must do it religiously, like practicing your putting! @JeffShavitz

_____

_____

_____

42

There are approximately 20MM golfers in the USA; find out how many golfers are located within 30 miles of your course. @JeffShavitz

_____

_____

_____

43

Rewards, awards, and golf giveaways to your golfing audience is an effective way to create loyalty. @JeffShavitz

_____

_____

_____

44

Is your course "that" different than other courses within a 20-mile radius? Execution will make the difference. @JeffShavitz

_____

_____

_____

SECTION III

Non-traditional Golf Course Revenue

Tee-time sales are the primary revenue source for golf course owners and executives. Think out of the box: there are many other services that can drive incremental revenue for your facility.

45

As Benjamin Franklin stated in 1748,
"Time is money." For the entrepreneur
and golf business owner, it definitely is!
@JeffShavitz

_____

_____

_____

46

Become friends with your competition.
It's a big world out there, so don't be
scared to share info with fellow golf
course operators. @JeffShavitz

_____

_____

_____

47

Partner with national golf advertising companies to sell more rounds for you. Why not call Clickit Golf? (I had to write this.) @JeffShavitz

_____

_____

_____

48

When was the last time you took a corporate retreat to think "out of the box" of how to grow your course? I would guess never! @JeffShavitz

_____

_____

_____

49

Clickitgolf, for no money out of pocket, will drive new golfers to your course.
@JeffShavitz

_____

_____

_____

50

A well-designed rewards program works
– why do you think the airlines and credit
card companies spend so much money
on them? @JeffShavitz

_____

_____

_____

51

Monthly raffles with great prizes incent
golfers to visit your course. A raffle to
the Masters and US Open – it works!
@JeffShavitz

_____

_____

_____

52

Speak for free at industry events,
universities, chambers – it's a great way
to meet local people in the community.
@JeffShavitz

_____

_____

_____

53

Develop marketing strategies to promote golf for the next generation of clients: children, women, seniors, etc. @JeffShavitz

_____

_____

_____

54

Golf marketing is combining a "people" solution with technology to gain business intelligence. @JeffShavitz

_____

_____

_____

55

Running local golf tournaments is a great way to add incremental revenue for your golf course. @JeffShavitz

_____

_____

_____

56

The golf database is a very valuable target audience for advertisers – have you ever sold advertising in your local market? @JeffShavitz

_____

_____

_____

57

Find your niche within the golf industry and then exploit it. You can't be everything to everyone. @JeffShavitz

_____

_____

_____

58

Try something completely different
and wacky this year for your business.
@JeffShavitz

_____

_____

_____

59

Start a formal golf referral program to get
new golfers. It's easy to do but you must do
it. @JeffShavitz

_____

_____

_____

60

No need to always invent a brand-new product or service. Just improve on something already in the golf marketplace. @JeffShavitz

_____

_____

_____

61

When was the last time you "wasted" some money on a new golfing concept for your course? I call it "investing." @JeffShavitz

_____

_____

_____

62

Learn in 60 seconds different
golf marketing techniques:
http://bit.ly/2fbpKaa @JeffShavitz

_____

_____

_____

63

Never let money be the obstacle for trying a
new business concept to grow your course.
A good idea will find capital. @JeffShavitz

_____

_____

_____

· SECTION ·

IV

Your Employees Matter

It's all about your people. Your employees should feel that their work is more than just a job. For this to happen, you must treat your employees with respect and empathy and build the right culture and vision.

64

Do you have the right people in your org? Tell yourself the truth: Should you fire somebody who doesn't fit your culture? @JeffShavitz

_____

_____

_____

65

Surround yourself with a management team that has different skill sets than yourself. @JeffShavitz

_____

_____

_____

66

When was the last time you invited a junior-level person of your company out for lunch just to listen to their ideas? @JeffShavitz

_____

_____

_____

67

Ensure that all your personnel understand the vision of your golf course. It sounds easy but it's really not. @JeffShavitz

_____

_____

_____

68

Nurture young adults with your golfing/ business culture; one day, they could possibly become your partner. @JeffShavitz

_____

_____

_____

69

As a business owner, I hate the annual holiday review period for employee raises and bonuses. My employees now expect it. @JeffShavitz

_____

_____

_____

70

If a specific employee is always calling in sick on Mondays and Fridays, are they really sick? Think about it. @JeffShavitz

_____

_____

_____

71

How can some employee ALWAYS finish their job at 5PM? Only if they start cleaning their desk at 4:45PM. Fire them. @JeffShavitz

_____

_____

_____

72

Hire slowly and fire quickly – best advice I ever learned from a human resources perspective. @JeffShavitz

_____

_____

_____

73

Treat all your people with respect and empathy. If you have a superstar employee, do you treat them differently? @JeffShavitz

_____

_____

_____

74

Do your due diligence before hiring someone. Of course their references will be good. Dig deeper. @JeffShavitz

_____

_____

_____

75

A honest, real, and authentic relationship with your golfing clientele will have them coming back for more rounds. @JeffShavitz

_____

_____

_____

76

When you interview employees, do you have a key question you always ask? And will that answer determine whether you hire them? @JeffShavitz

_____

_____

_____

77

Many people have different aspirations, interests & skill sets. This is good, or everyone would want to be the golf executive. @JeffShavitz

_____

_____

_____

78

Invest money and time into your employees. Invest in your facility. Company morale amongst your team is critical to success. @JeffShavitz

_____

_____

_____

79

Empathy is a very powerful word, whether playing golf or running a golf course. Respect everyone. @JeffShavitz

_____

_____

_____

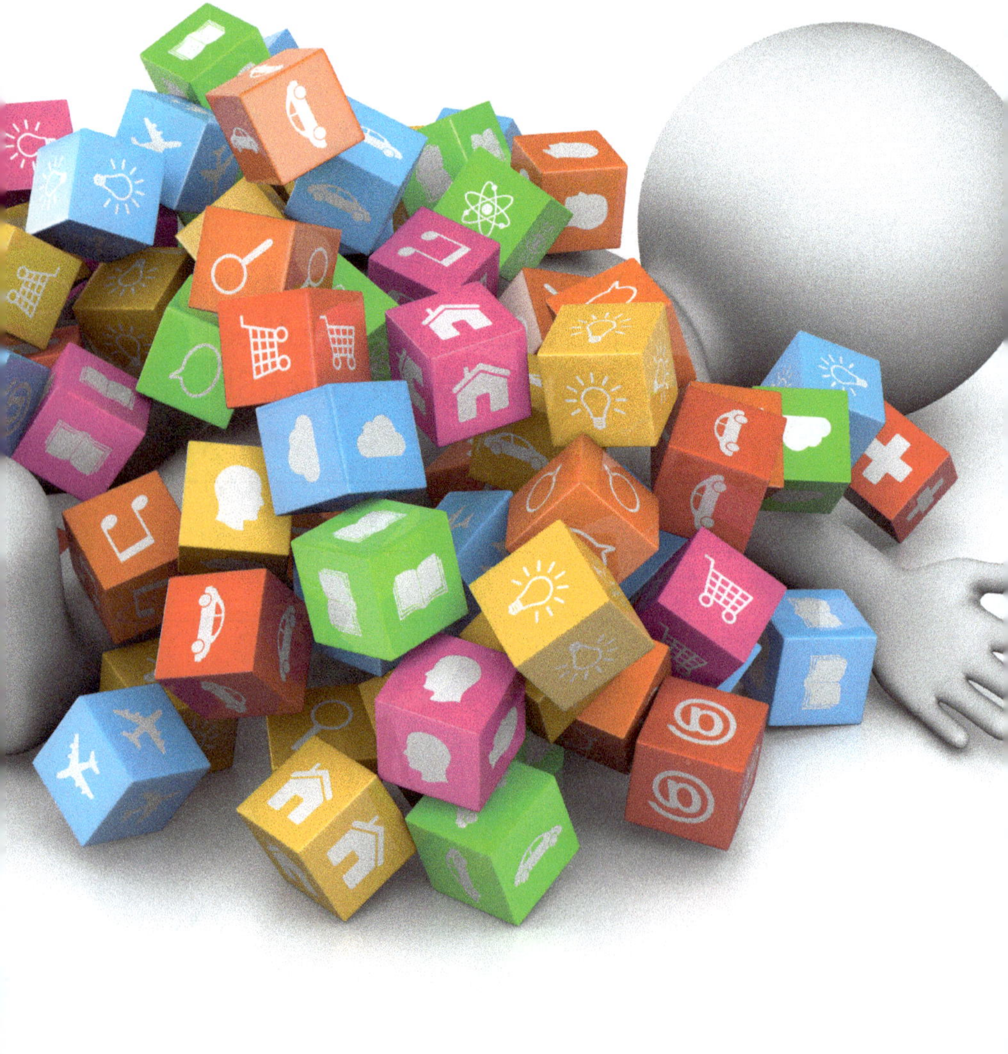

· SECTION ·

V

Don't Be Afraid of Technology

Obvious statement: social media and technology integration will only increase with golf courses and golfers to make the golf experience more enjoyable. Embrace and learn technology and watch your round sales increase.

80

Speak in "your voice" to your customer via social. Don't just copy and paste content from another website. @JeffShavitz

_____

_____

_____

81

Be consistent in your social media posts – once a day, once per week, once per month, whatever it is – stick to the schedule. @JeffShavitz

_____

_____

_____

82

Hire a social media consultant to help you get your social media posts done regularly. @JeffShavitz

_____

_____

_____

83

What strategies are you implementing to keep existing golfers coming back to your course? @JeffShavitz

_____

_____

_____

84

In today's world, you must use lots of marketing strategies to reach your golfers, as there are many ways to find your course. @JeffShavitz

_____

_____

_____

85

Do you have a social media app? If not, get one quickly or you are losing many sales. @JeffShavitz

_____

_____

_____

86

Use Facebook, Twitter, and other social media to promote special offers for your course. @JeffShavitz

_____

_____

_____

87

Hire a millennial to run your social media. Or outsource it. But somebody must be accountable to getting it done daily! @JeffShavitz

_____

_____

_____

88

When was the last time you updated your website? If over 6 months, it probably needs a refresh. @JeffShavitz

_____

_____

_____

89

When did you last quantify the results of your last marketing campaign? Was it a gut reaction that "worked" or "didn't work"? @JeffShavitz

_____

_____

_____

90

Don't forget to add the "waste money expense line item" into your budget. With this money, try cool stuff to promote growth. @JeffShavitz

_____

_____

_____

91

Start writing a blog on the golf industry – even if nobody reads it, you can say that you are a golf blog author! @JeffShavitz

_____

_____

_____

92

Back up all your important passwords and computer logins. For $.99, you can use an iPhone application. Good investment! @JeffShavitz

_____

_____

_____

93

For the "older" generation of golf executives, learn about social media. Have you heard of Facebook and Twitter? @JeffShavitz

_____

_____

_____

94

Millennials want to use technology to book
tee times. Use it, learn it, and embrace it!
@JeffShavitz

_____

_____

_____

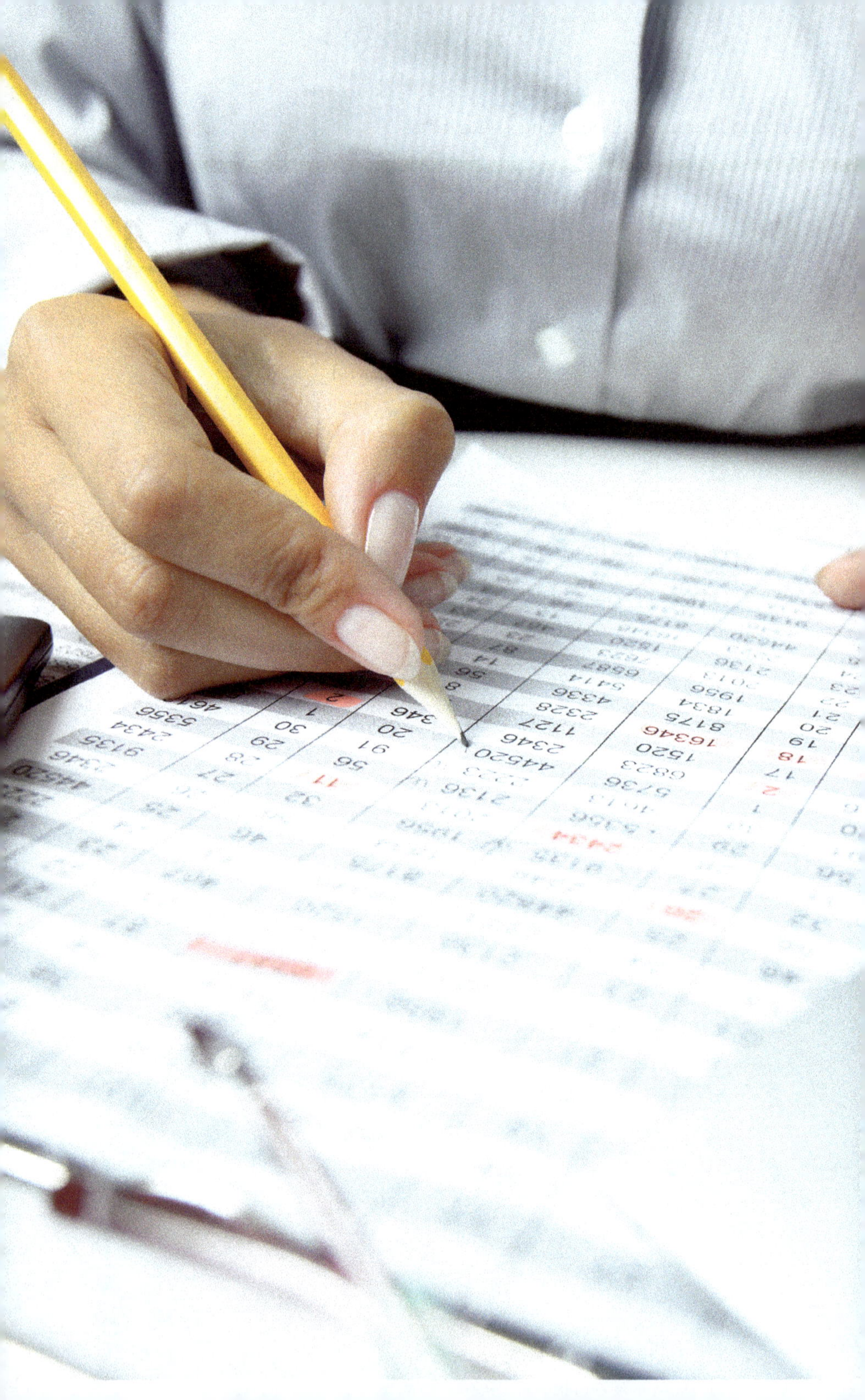

· S E C T I O N ·

VI

Know Your Numbers

It's all about the numbers, as your accountant will tell you—your financials, your budgets, your profitability, your prospect lists, and the cost to acquire a customer. Without understanding your numbers, you will not understand your golf course as a business.

95

The industry of golf is stagnant - what does that mean? It doesn't mean that YOUR golf course can't grow. @JeffShavitz

_____

_____

_____

96

It's not just about the money. But the net profit is the scorecard of how well your facility is doing. @JeffShavitz

_____

_____

_____

97

50% of start-up companies fail within a few years. When did your golf course open?
@JeffShavitz

_____

_____

_____

98

Know your numbers: Successful business people know every month how their company is doing (and it's not just a gut feeling). @JeffShavitz

_____

_____

_____

99

Big data is not just for Fortune 500 companies. Analytics, metrics & buying patterns of your golfers are critical for success. @JeffShavitz

_____

_____

_____

100

Facts & numbers don't lie – you can't make it up. Running your golf course is like running any company. Do monthly budgets.
@JeffShavitz

_____

_____

_____

101

Do your customers, golf pros, part-time help & full-time employees really know what you are thinking? Share with them. @JeffShavitz

_____

_____

_____

102

As a business owner, understand your credit card fees. There are many "hidden fees" that will decrease your profitability. @JeffShavitz

_____

_____

_____

103

Monthly planning: Do you honestly know if your golf course made or lost money last month? Last week? Study your numbers.
@JeffShavitz

_____

_____

_____

104

Work an extra hour per day. Assuming 270 work days per year, that's 270 hours, which is another 39 work days a year. @JeffShavitz

_____

_____

_____

105

When was the last time you reviewed your 1-year, 3-year, or 5-year plan? Do you even have a plan for next month? @JeffShavitz

_____

_____

_____

106

Forget the three-year plan – write down three things you want to accomplish this month. And then do them. @JeffShavitz

_____

_____

_____

107

Know financial ratios – debt to equity, EBITDA, liquidity – and understand accounting or hire financial people to help you. @JeffShavitz

_____

_____

_____

108

Receive a daily mgt report highlighting your daily sales – you better know your #s and have a pulse on your company! @JeffShavitz

_____

_____

_____

109

Review monthly bank & credit card statements. Whether or not you have a CFO, you need to understand your cash flow.
@JeffShavitz

_____

_____

_____

110

How many hours do you work a day as a golf course owner? It never stops, right?
@JeffShavitz

_____

_____

_____

SECTION VII

AHAs to Think About

Becoming a successful golf owner is difficult. Sleepless nights. Daily fires. Employee issues. Payroll. Lots to think about. A growing "to do" list. Enjoy these AHAs that will help you introspectively think about the future of your golf business.

111

A commodity can always be sold at a lower price. Your golf course is not a commodity. @JeffShavitz

_____

_____

_____

112

Why did you want to own a golf course?
Owning and playing golf are two very
different things. @JeffShavitz

113

Why do otherwise sane men and women
ever take up the life of the entrepreneur
and running a golf course vs. corporate
America? @JeffShavitz

114

Don't text and drive on the way to the golf course. Everything can wait. Be a responsible human being. @JeffShavitz

_____

_____

_____

115

Do the things you hate doing first thing in the morning to get them over with! @JeffShavitz

_____

_____

_____

116

Did you ever have a business "AHA moment" to grow your golf course? Act on it. @JeffShavitz

_____

_____

_____

117

Think about what "money" really means to you. It's a personal answer. Your golf course will prospect quicker depending on the answer. @JeffShavitz

_____

_____

_____

118

When was the last time you had a great idea for your facility but were lazy and did nothing about it? @JeffShavitz

_____

_____

_____

119

If you own a golf course, you can give yourself any title you like & any green or fairway as your office! @JeffShavitz

_____

_____

_____

120

What drives you for success? Is it only money? Be introspective and really understand your answer. @JeffShavitz

_____

_____

_____

121

Most people are jealous of your success. Only ask people for advice whom you truly trust and respect. @JeffShavitz

_____

_____

_____

122

Do you have a business mentor to bounce ideas off of? Or a board of directors to get feedback on the sanity of your concepts? @JeffShavitz

_____

_____

_____

123

Do you belong to a business group and meet on a monthly business to network and learn? @JeffShavitz

_____

_____

_____

124

Network with people "NOT" like yourself.
It's too easy to always surround yourself
with people who share similar backgrounds.
@JeffShavitz

_____

_____

_____

125

Why do you work so hard? There must be
a reason. For me, it's "freedom." What's your
answer? @JeffShavitz

_____

_____

_____

126

Surprise your SO and/or children – take the day off for no reason to spend quality time with them. The pro shop will be fine. @JeffShavitz

_____

_____

_____

127

Balance in life is important. Develop a passion/hobby outside of golf that you are really committed to. If not, find one.
@JeffShavitz

_____

_____

_____

128

Establish a "no work zone" in your home –
don't always talk shop with your partner or
significant other, it gets boring. @JeffShavitz

_____

_____

_____

129

Are you happy with the combination of your
business and personal life? Just give a "yes"
or "no" answer. @JeffShavitz

_____

_____

_____

130

Take 3 slow breaths at work every day.
It will make for a more effective work day!
Also works when you putt under pressure.
@JeffShavitz

_____

_____

_____

131

Don't leave your pro shop until you have written down your plan and to-do list for the following day. @JeffShavitz

_____

_____

_____

132

We all have different priorities and your values matter – never deviate from your personal mission with your golf facility. @JeffShavitz

_____

_____

_____

133

What is your personality trait? Type A?
Good guess. @JeffShavitz

_____

_____

_____

134

Yoga, although I'm terrible at it,
has become an enjoyable hour for me.
You need downtime from the craziness
of the course. @JeffShavitz

_____

_____

_____

135

Read a business book (not a golf book) this
week – if not the whole book, then at least
the back cover to learn something new!
@JeffShavitz

_____

_____

_____

136

Read my book, "Size Doesn't Matter." Great info for the small to mid-size business owner, whether golf-related or not. @JeffShavitz

_____

_____

_____

137

Make yourself feel vulnerable and get out of your comfort zone. You'll feel alive, and your golf course will thrive. @JeffShavitz

_____

_____

_____

138

There is an expression, "Don't judge a book by its cover." I disagree; a first impression is an everlasting impression. @JeffShavitz

_____

_____

_____

139

It's a trite expression to "learn from your failures." But it's true. Rory learned from his loss in the 2011 Masters. @JeffShavitz

_____

_____

_____

140

My favorite business quote: "The harder you work, the luckier you become." It's true. It's like practicing on the range. @JeffShavitz

_____

_____

_____

About the Author

Jeff Shavitz loves everything about the game of golf (while wishing he had a lower handicap) and is excited about acquiring Clickitgolf Inc. in 2016.

Jeff is a successful entrepreneur, having started and sold three companies prior to entering the golf business. As Jeff states, "business is business," and the same principles prevail, whether owning a golf course or running other types of companies.

Jeff is a successful business book author with five published books; his first book, *Size Doesn't Matter — Why Small Business Is BIG Business*, hit number one on Amazon. He is a national speaker and contributing writer for *Entrepreneur Magazine*, *The Business Journal*, and other business publications.

Jeff received his Bachelor of Arts degree in Economics from Tufts University and spent one semester at the London School of Economics, specializing in finance. He is very involved in many business, civic, and philanthropic organizations, including the Young Presidents' Organization. Jeff's selfish goal is to play the top 100 golf courses in the USA.

AHAthat™

AHAthat makes it easy to share, author, and promote content. There are over 38,000 quotes (AHAmessages™) by thought leaders from around the world that you can share in seconds for free.

For those who want to author their own book, we have time-tested proven processes that allow you to write your AHAbook™ of 140 digestible, bite-sized morsels in eight hours or less. Once your content is on AHAthat, you have a customized link that you can use to have your fans/advocates share your content and help grow your network.

➲ Start sharing: http://AHAthat.com

➲ Start authoring: http://AHAthat.com/author

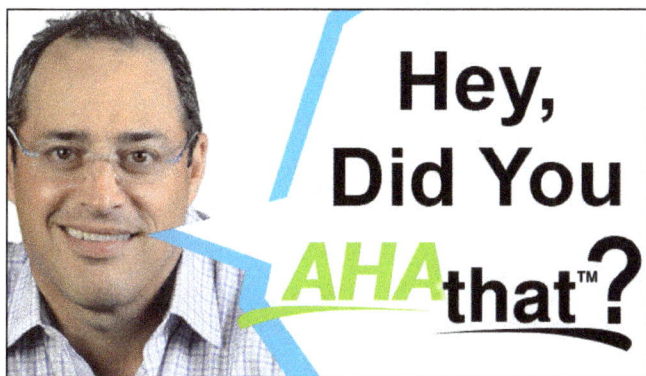

Please go directly to this book in AHAthat and share each AHAmessage socially at http://aha.pub/GolfCourseRev.

www.ingramcontent.com/pod-product-compliance
Lightning Source LLC
Chambersburg PA
CBHW060546100426
42742CB00013B/2467